Dare To Be Holy

Dare To Be Holy

*One Man's Journey
to Practical Holiness*

Bill Wegner
with
Thomas A. Szyszkiewicz

Foreword by Jeff Cavins

All direct Scripture quotations are taken from The Holy Bible, Revised
Standard Version, Catholic Edition, © 1965, Thomas Nelson & Sons.

ISBN 0-9771859-0-7

Cover art by Karen Wasielewski

Visit us on our website at: http://goodnewsinternational.net

To my wife, Cheryl,
my gift from God.

Contents

Acknowledgments

I would like to thank my co-author, Tom Szyszkiewicz, for helping me take my spoken words and putting them on paper. I struggled for many years to try to do that. Thank you to Ana Maria Garcia for being my editor and critic. And I mean that in a good way.

A real big thank you to my ministry friends and teachers, David Stewart, Charlie Osborn, Brian Casey, "Big John" Schweisthal, Joe Williams and especially my partner in ministry, Brent Heiser, who taught me more than he will ever know and who put up with me for 10 years on the road. Thanks guys for letting me "borrow" all your material for this book.

I must also acknowledge and thank Johnnette Benkovic, Jeff Cavins, Ralph Martin, George McGovern and Joe Klecko for their friendship, encouragement and for their kind words about the book. And, of course, all of my gratitude goes to Father Brendan Williams, my pastor, spiritual director and good friend.

A special thanks to Peter Grandich whose friendship and support made this book possible. And of course to my family. To my mom, Mary, for always praying for me as St. Monica did for St. Augustine. Thanks, Mom. To my beautiful kids Brian, Amy, Erin and Kati, I love you all so much. To my grandsons Riley, Dylan and Samuel and to the two other grandkids on the way, thanks for keeping me young (at heart, at least, if not in looks).

The biggest thanks of all to my best friend and the love of my life, Cheryl, for living most of this book with me and for sticking with me when a lot wouldn't and didn't. I thank God for you each day.

Foreword

Over the last thirty years I have had the privilege of meeting many people who have dedicated their lives to the work of the Lord. There is something attractive about holiness and complete dedication, something desirable. Mother Theresa is an example of a life given totally to Christ and she continues to inspire and change lives today. Holiness is the challenge and privilege to be different. But being different isn't the goal itself; rather being different is the privilege of being like Jesus. The world desperately needs Jesus Christ; therefore the world desperately needs you to be different.

A person's testimony is a powerful tool in the hands of God. As Americans we tend to hold our cards close to our chest, we don't often disclose the inner workings of our hearts. When we do let others into our life we take a risk, a risk that many find difficult. The Apostle Paul took such risks as he painted the Gospel on the canvas of his own life. Admitting his strengths and weaknesses, he became accessible to his audience and became a living demonstration of the drama between God and man. In *Dare To Be Holy*, Bill Wegner opens his life up to us in such a way that we can not only see the way God worked in his life, but we can begin to imagine the ways in which God can move in ours.

I have known Bill for several years and have a deep respect for his humble and transparent heart. There are not many who would give up what others consider the American Dream to go and travel the world's highways and back roads with the message of the Gospel. What would move a man and his family to pursue the Lord so faithfully year in and year out? That is the content of this book.

The late Pope John Paul II said that the *New Evangelization* is almost impossible without the laity. Bill Wegner's story is an example of how the laity can change the world if they keep their focus on the vision set forth by the King of kings. You will be inspired and challenged to grow in holiness as a result of reading *Dare to Be Holy*.

Jeff Cavins

Co-Author's Preface

In helping Bill Wegner write this book, I had a couple of personal revelations: 1) Holiness does not necessarily look like what we might think it looks like, and 2) holiness is hard to achieve, grates on our nerves, is a real pain in the neck, and dislodges us out of our comfort zones.

Let me elaborate. Many of us think holiness looks only like Mother Teresa or Padre Pio – someone from a foreign country who was either a priest or a religious and who naturally exuded goodness effortlessly. (I'm sure you would be at least a little forgiving if either one of them got a little irritated with you and told you that their lives were burdened with great suffering and clinging to the Lord was never easy.)

But we will not generally think of a married man who grew up in Newark, New Jersey, as someone who is holy unless he was working with the poor or became widowed and then went into the monastery. However, Bill teaches some very strong and hard lessons in what God conceives of as holy. I don't think he would claim that he has attained any great sanctity himself, and rightly so. But I can tell you that some of the things he has done in his life were truly holy actions, actions that really reflected the fact that he, by the grace of Baptism, is set aside for God. And they are actions that I don't know if I could do.

Those holy actions are the ones that are most difficult to do and really dislodge us out of our comfort zone. We've all heard about those whose loved ones have been killed by some idiot and have had the courage and ability to offer forgiveness to that person. Well, you can read about an episode in Bill's life that is similar. I guarantee it will not be easy reading and your mind will probably start exploding with questions about the justice of what he believed God required of him, like mine did. I'd encourage you to wrestle with those questions and bring them to God and a good spiritual director.

Or you can find out about really difficult people in your life and what the Lord demands of us when we relate to them.

When we gave the subtitle to this book, we wanted people to know that holiness is not simply a pious look on the face. Rather, it is very practical. When Mother Teresa was picking up people out of the dingy streets of Calcutta, she did not necessarily look pious, but her practical efforts brought her to holiness. When Padre Pio received the stigmata, there was a very practical effect to it – a lot of pain. And when he received the gift of reading hearts in the confessional, it was very practical advice he gave to the penitents.

When we look at the Sermon on the Mount, Jesus is giving us concrete things to do – do not judge; ask, seek, knock; do not sound a trumpet when you give alms; leave your gift at the altar and be reconciled with your brother; let your yes be yes and your no be no; turn the other cheek; if someone takes your coat, give him your cloak as well. The problem comes when we think this is too crazy and don't follow what he says.

I write this out of my own experience. Bill asked me to help him with this book because I'm a writer, not a saint. As I've worked on the book, I've come to realize how little I have obtained in the way of holiness and that it's primarily an issue of obedience to God's word. "Fathers, do not nag your children lest they lose heart," St. Paul says, not once, but twice. Hmmm, something to do there. "Husbands, love your wives as Christ loved the Church." Another action step to take.

As you read this book, take to heart what God is saying to you and to all – that if we do as he tells us, then we will truly be happy.

Thomas A. Szyszkiewicz

Preface

There's a great story I heard once. A Navy captain saw the lights of another vessel heading toward him. So he said to his signalman, "Send this message: Change your course 10 degrees south."

The signalman sent the message and he got one back – but not what he was expecting. "Change your course 10 degrees north."

So the captain said, "What kind of garbage is that? Tell him, 'I am a captain. Change your course 10 degrees south.'"

The reply came, "I am a seaman third class. Change your course 10 degrees north."

The captain went ballistic. "I can't believe the insolence of this – this –. Send this, 'You idiot! Change your course 10 degrees south. I am on a battleship.'"

And this reply came back: "Change your course 10 degrees north. I am in a lighthouse."

I'm just like that captain. I'm always the one who wants to be in charge. I'm always the one who thinks he's right. I'm always the one that wants the lighthouse to move. I'm always the one who thinks he can do it better.

Obviously, life doesn't work that way, does it? There's someone else who *is* in charge, someone else who *is* always right, someone else who *can* do it the best.

And when you *think* you're in charge, always right and the best, you're going to run into problems when you come up against that someone else who actually *is*.

That, in a nutshell, is the story of my life, which I want to share with you in this book. We all have our own testimonies about how God has worked in our lives, where he has miraculously intervened and helped us out, shown us the light that doesn't move, like the lighthouse.

But what I want to do in this book is to share my testimony in light of the Sermon on the Mount, as it's known in Matthew's Gospel (Matt. 5-7), and the Sermon on the Plain, as it's known in Luke's Gospel (6:17-49).

In this sermon, Jesus sets out what the Kingdom of God is like, and it sets the values of the world upside down on their heads. He gives us the Beatitudes, the blessings we receive as His followers when we are poor and meek, mourn, hunger and thirst for righteousness, show mercy, are pure of heart and peacemakers. He also commands us to love our enemies, do good to those who hate us, turn the other cheek, give our shirt if our cloak is taken, and give to everyone who begs of us.

These are not the values of the world. The values of the world are listed in St. Paul's letter to the Galatians: "fornication, uncleanness, lewdness, idolatry, sorcery, enmities, strife, jealousy, anger, rivalry, divisions, sects, envy, drunkenness, reveling and the like." But Paul goes on to make it really clear that you can't engage in such behavior and expect to be in the kingdom of God. "I warn you as I warned you before, those who do such things will not inherit the kingdom of God." (Gal. 5:20-21)

O.K., I'll admit it. I engaged in a lot of these things before my conversion. Oh, I was a Catholic, at least I was baptized one. But was I living a Christian life? Not by any stretch of the imagination.

However, God, in his mercy, reached out and touched my life. And fortunately for me, it happened before I got into any really serious trouble – like going to prison and dying there, which happened to a business partner of mine.

Now, I'm not going to tell you everything about me and for two very good reasons. The first is obvious – you wouldn't want to know everything about me. The second is that if you really knew me – and I mean everything about me, what I've done, what I've thought, what I've said – then you wouldn't want to read this book. But you know what else I've learned? If I really knew you, I wouldn't want to write it for you.

That's the great thing about life in God. We know we're all sinners, we're all in need of his mercy and help. And what you're about to read is one man's story about how God gave that mercy and help.

Bill Wegner

Chapter 1

Life in Newark

Newark, New Jersey. That city's name doesn't exactly excite you, does it? Some people say that it's an ugly city with all kinds of factories, abandoned buildings, pollution and high crime. Some people say it's a good place to "be from." But for the first fourteen years of my life, that's where I grew up. And believe it or not, it was a great place to do that.

At home, I had three parents. Yes, that's right, I said three parents. My father, also named William, was from rural Minnesota. My mother, Mary Rose (nee) Lynch, was from Newark. And my third parent was Bridget Theresa Lynch, my mom's mom, who lived with us. I was the oldest of four children. Judy, my sister was two years younger than me. Bobby was born eleven months after Judy, they called them "Irish twins" in those days. And then there was Tommy, born sixteen years after I was. I don't know what they called that.

Mom and Dad met during World War II and couldn't have been more different – Dad was a rural Midwestern Republican; Mom was an urban Democrat. But what brought them and kept them together was their strong Catholic faith. Mom and Grandma were Irish Catholic (Grandma had grown up in Ireland and moved to the U.S. when she was 17 or 18). Dad grew up in a very

Protestant area of Minnesota where a traveling priest would come by every four to six weeks to celebrate Mass. Because of that background, church was a big part of our lives.

Newark was great. During the summer, my friends and I would go to the Boyland Street pool and spend the whole day there only taking our towels and bathing suits and, if we were lucky, *maybe* a dollar. We'd leave at eight or nine in the morning and not get home until seven or eight at night. Or we'd get on a bus and go downtown to the movies on a Saturday or just hang around.

School was not that difficult for me – I always did pretty well in it. I had the usual social pressures of growing up at that time, mainly trying to find the right group and trying to be a good kid so I didn't embarrass my parents. Fortunately, we had none of the pressures then that kids have today – no need to worry about sex, drugs or alcohol. Oh sure, there were some kids who did that, but it was a shadowy thing for us and not something we wanted any part of.

Actually, I think the best part about growing up in Newark was my parish and school, St. Antoninus, which was staffed by Dominican priests and the Sisters of Charity. Three young priests especially stick in my mind: Fathers Jim Core, Tom Eartle and Owen Beatty. These guys were my heroes. They were three smiling, happy, well-adjusted young men who had a relationship with God, who were great preachers – and they loved us kids.

I so admired these guys that I thought I would become one of them. It was more than that, actually. I thought I had a vocation – a calling to the priesthood. I got some information from some orders and the Sacred Heart Fathers in Cincinnati had the best-looking brochure, so I decided I would go to high school seminary there. Mind you, I was about 13-years-old at the time and there was something I was obviously lacking – experience in the world. The Sacred Heart Fathers sent a representative to interview me and the priest asked me a lot of really personal questions, questions that I really had no answer to because I had no clue what he was talking about.

That didn't faze me, though. I told the Dominicans at the parish that I was going to the seminary. It must have been something I said, because all three of them ended up on our doorstep – to talk me out of doing it! They knew me and they knew I didn't have a vocation and that I wasn't ready for the rigors of seminary.

"Excuse me," I asked them, "are you trying to talk me out of this, Fathers?"

"Yeah, we're trying to talk you into getting some life experience and *then* going ahead with it. If God's calling you, he doesn't care if you wait until after high school.

He'll still be there and you'll still have a vocation. So just wait."

I've often reflected back on that and thought how wise and how good God was to send me these three young men, whom I so respected, loved and admired. I don't know if there was anybody else who could have deterred me from going into the seminary – and probably making a very large mistake.

Chapter 2

Our move to the 'burbs

During this time, Newark was changing. This was the beginning of the mass move to the suburbs, and a lot of my friends were going. In their place came criminal types and we now had to worry about walking down the street. Burglaries, muggings, police cruisers – all of these started to become more common. Gangs started to rise up as well, and my friends and I started to get into that kind of stuff.

My dad saw what was going on and didn't like it. "It's time for us to get out of the city," he said. It wasn't only the city problems – Mom and Dad also wanted to buy a house. So we started making weekend excursions to Monmouth County to do house hunting. Eventually, we found one, in Neptune Township, New Jersey. Shark River Hills to be exact.

It was in an area that hadn't really developed yet – the streets were unpaved and there were no streetlights. It was not much of a house, really. It was a three-bedroom with one bathroom and moving into it were three adults and three children.

But, to a family who had lived in an apartment in a three-family home in Newark, this was great. We thought we had died and gone to heaven. We actually had a shower!

The adjustment at first was not an easy one for me, particularly for school. But I got through those initial pains and my four years at St. Rose High School in Belmar were wonderful.

This was the beginning of my interest in work, politics and golf, which would follow me for the rest of my life – I worked at McDonald's, at a supermarket and my dad got me a job as a caddy. Mom and Dad would really go at it discussing politics and I usually ended up agreeing with my Mom.

And, of course, there was a love interest. I had a girlfriend named Mary.

In spite of all this, though, I really had no idea what I was going to do with my life. (That may have had something to do with the fact that I was starting to party a lot, too.) But when you have no idea where you're going, people will ply you with all kinds of suggestions. The main one I got was, "Why don't you go into education?" The reasoning was that they always needed men in teaching and they can go on to be the administrators.

And because I completely lacked direction, I said, "Well, maybe I'll do that," and I went to college to become an elementary school teacher.

Chapter 3
Becoming all-knowing

A wonderful thing happened to me when I went off to college – I became all-knowing. Yes, it was an amazing thing but I came to know all things and everything I knew was 100% correct. What a miracle!

Not that anyone noticed. But in those days, I began to discover that I had it all figured out, and that my parents, teachers, priests and just about everybody over thirty were surprisingly stupid. I actually felt sorry for them. They were so dumb and didn't seem to know it.

My first semester was easy. I got a 3.0 and I didn't do any work. It got harder after that and I started to put in some effort. In my day (1966-1970) there was one big motivator to be in college and to stay there – to avoid the draft and stay out of Vietnam. I did what I had to do so I wouldn't fail and be kicked out. If that happened, I would instantly be classified 1A.

I joined a fraternity, surviving the disgusting things they put us through during the pledge time. The group I joined boasted of having a keg of beer available 24/7. They were a rather athletic group of guys as well, and I enjoyed that a lot.

The athletic thing kind of expanded into other areas. My fraternity brothers and I would frequently go to a luncheonette nearby and get football tickets from guys with slicked back hair and sharkskin suits. These tickets were completely illegal, of course, and were a gambling venture for the sharkskins. This was small-time stuff, but it was my real start into the world of gambling.

College during the mid-1960s was a tumultuous time. The war, civil rights, drugs, assassinations, riots, demonstrations, killing of students by the National Guard, "free" love. It was a time when we really started accepting degradation, perversion and sin, and calling it by every other name – love, caring, service.

We were told as young people that it was our job to change America through protests, sex, drugs and rock-and-roll. As long as it doesn't hurt anybody, it's OK, we were told.

I bought into the whole mentality hook, line and sinker. Of course, most of my professors did the same and they were brilliant and my college friends were brilliant. And, therefore, because I hung around with them, I was absolutely brilliant, too.

That's when the superior attitude developed. Wow! My parents suddenly became dumb – how did they get to be so dumb? And the Church? How did it get so out of step with the rest of the real world? The government? They were just mean, nasty and corrupt.

My brilliance got to my head, of course. If I'm so brilliant, why did I need God? I didn't! I didn't need God. I didn't need the Church. They were totally irrelevant. It just wasn't *sophisticated* to have a relationship with God.

So I didn't. And from that single decision you can see for yourself how a lot of things did not go the way they should have gone, beginning with marriage.

Chapter 4
Marriage

One day while I was living at home, but still going to college, I got a call. It was my old high school girlfriend, Mary. We hadn't seen each other for a couple of years.

"Why are you calling?" I asked. "I heard you were getting married."

"Well, I've been thinking about you for quite a while. I *am* supposed to get married, but I decided I would call you to see how you felt about me and if there was any chance we could have a relationship. If not, then I'll go ahead and get married to this guy."

I found that very interesting. We decided to go ahead and start up our relationship again. But I found out later that my Mom, who was listening in on the conversation, wasn't happy. Neither was my Dad. And her family was unhappy as well.

That was not a very good start to something, but we forged ahead and two years later, after we graduated from college, we got married. Why? Well, because we wanted to even though almost everyone, friends and family alike, could see we weren't very compatible. I didn't care what everyone thought. I thought I was in love and that was all that mattered.

Not a smart move. I came from a fairly stable family, my parents had been married for over twenty years at that time, but Mary's family – well that was a different story. Mary was one of seven children, but her father was an active alcoholic and gone from the house, leaving her mother to raise them by herself. Most families are dysfunctional to some degree. Really, what is "normal"? But Mary's family had more than its share of dysfunction. Looking back, I really think I wanted to rescue her from that situation and I did that by marrying her.

Things were OK when we first started our marriage. We were both working. We were buying furniture and starting to build a life together. We were both elementary school teachers. We could get by on the two salaries and working in the summer. But then Mary wanted to have children right away. She got pregnant, quit work, and we were stuck on my first-year teacher's salary – less than seven thousand dollars. Even in 1971 that was pretty bad.

Our son Brian John Wegner was born in July of 1972 – it was wonderful to be a father and to watch him being born. What a miracle! And I felt that even though it would be a struggle, everything was going to be fine from then on.

But it wasn't. These two Catholic High School kids who used to go to Mass together, who got married in the Catholic Church – we no longer had God in our lives. He wasn't sophisticated enough for us.

I was hoping that now that we had Brian, we could both get back to work, save some money and maybe buy a house. We were poor and I hated it. We had no money for anything extra. We couldn't go out. We could hardly even entertain friends at home. I remember that in those days I used to smoke and most times could not afford to buy a pack of cigarettes and they were a lot less expensive than they are now.

As time went on we disagreed about practically everything. Our marriage was in trouble. Because we had no God in our lives and because most everyone had advised against the marriage in the first place, I at least felt we had no place to turn for help. I did not want to hear "I told you so." Mary became pregnant for the second time. We argued a lot more than we did before. When Amy Elizabeth was born, it was great – a miracle all over again. She was absolutely beautiful. But the stress of the constant fighting was too much and we decided to separate.

That was horrible. By the time Amy was being baptized, we weren't even living together. I was racked every single day with guilt. Here I was, the first person in my family to graduate from college and I was also the first person to get divorced.

I spent a lot of time trying to drink away the pain. I took a full-time job as a bartender in addition to being a teacher. Now that I had to pay child support, I needed the money even more than before. But I also felt I needed the environment – the drinking and the partying, which I did plenty of with my teacher friends – because I wanted to forget.

All during the separation and eventual divorce, I spent lots of time with Brian and Amy, seeing them on the weekends and at times during the week. It was good quality time, but it wasn't what God had intended.

Chapter 5

Temptation

You know what I've realized about my life? The only sins I haven't committed are the ones I haven't been tempted enough to do.

I found that out when I left teaching. In my seven years in that profession, I had been involved with the union, which meant I wasn't in the good graces of the administration. I also saw in those seven years that most – not all, but most – of the older teachers hated teaching and were burned out. I was only 31 and I didn't want to spend the next twenty-five years just waiting to retire.

I was bartending on the weekends at a luxury hotel, part of a major chain. A full-time job opened up there and I applied and got it. In thirty days, I got a raise and was making more than I had in seven years of teaching.

It was a lot of work, putting in fifteen, sixteen or more hours a day – and I loved it. A lot of times I'd just stay overnight at the hotel and do it again the next day.

The hotel management was duly impressed with my work ethic and I was made an assistant manager.

Brian and Amy were impressed, too. They would visit me there on the weekends and they had a lot of fun. We'd go swimming and have dinner in the fancy restaurant and they'd get the royal treatment from the hotel staff.

But I don't think God was impressed. If you had asked me what my religion was then and if I had been honest with you, I would have had to tell you that I was a total practicing heathen. And I was passing that on to my children as well.

For all that work, though, I thought my pay was on the small side. Oh, there were perks – my dry cleaning, gas and food were all free. Yet I saw these people in the hotel who had a lot of money and no one knew why – they had no visible means of support. And that started to gnaw at me and I started to think, "You know, I want to get some money. I work hard. I *deserve* it."

A priest friend told me later on in my life that he found it amazing that God puts some obvious limits on our intelligence, but none on our stupidity. That's my story exactly. I got to be as stupid as I wanted to be.

One day, I approached this guy that I'd gotten to be friends with, whom I'll call Richard. "I know what your background is," I told him. "I know you used to be a bookie when you were much younger. Are you interested in doing that again?"

Richard was a bit wary. "What do you mean?"

"Are you interested in getting back into the gambling business?" I said.

"With *you*?"

"Yeah, I think I'd like to do that."

"You know how dangerous that is, don't you?"

" Tell me."

"Well, the State of New Jersey is not very kind to people who do things like that. They don't like the competition 'cause they're in the gambling business themselves with the lotteries and casinos. So if you get caught, you're going to go to jail."

"Let's try to do it on a limited basis and we'll see what happens," I said, because my desire to have money overshadowed my fear of getting caught.

Of course, I can look back now and tell myself what a moron I was for doing that. I could have ruined my whole life by being sent to jail. At the very least, I would have embarrassed my parents and children, but more likely, I would have ruined their lives, too. I would have been a totally different person.

But I didn't think about any of that. Like most of the decisions I had made in my life up to this point – like getting married and divorced – I did it because *I* wanted to do it. I didn't worry at all what the consequences would be.

Richard had a lot of contacts and I had a few myself, so we set up shop. If you wanted to bet on a football or basketball game or just about anything else, we were the guys to call. For the next couple of years, we made quite a bit of money and I thought it was just plain fun. I love sports, particularly football. It's exciting for me to watch the games and it's even more exciting – whether you win or lose – when you have a $25,000 bet on the game.

Of course, all we needed was one or two people to get mad at us and turn us in, but I never stopped to think about that.

The only way I got out of the bookmaking business was by an act of God's mercy courtesy of the hotel I worked for, where I was now manager. One of the company's hotels just outside of Boston was having difficulty because the manager was doing a lousy job. When the regional manager went up for a visit, the hotel manager took a sudden leave of absence because of illness. That left the job open at a hotel that was twice the size of the one I was at and that was doing a tremendous amount of business. They offered me the job and I took it with the proviso that no matter what happened, I would get every other weekend off to see my kids. They agreed and I was off to Boston.

Richard didn't fare so well. After I left, he went a little crazy. He got arrested at the very hotel I used to manage, not for gambling but for selling drugs. Because he was so well "connected," the police had been watching him for a long time. After he was arrested he either wouldn't or couldn't give them the information they wanted, so for his drug conviction he was given life in prison, thirty years, no parole. At his age, it was a death sentence. And he died in Trenton State Prison. I used to visit him there.

Chapter 6

"Over my dead body"

I was sent to Boston on a temporary basis – my bosses gave me six months to a year to clean up the mess there – but it gave me a rather permanent change in my life, one I never would have imagined.

The move there was really difficult because I missed Brian and Amy a lot. I felt a tremendous amount of guilt and anxiety about the divorce and about how it was affecting them. I thought about them everyday and when the time came to leave on the weekends that we visited, I hated it.

A lot of divorced guys I knew didn't have the same feelings – they were almost glad to be rid of their roles as fathers. But that was simply inconceivable to me that a man would eradicate his children from his life. That was why I insisted that the company I worked for fly me home on as many weekends as possible.

Along with this burden was the difficulty of working at the hotel. The guy I was replacing wasn't all that willing to be replaced. He had been uncontrollably spending money and hiring his friends at exorbitant salaries. Those friends were still there and he'd call them to find out what I was doing. Then he had the nerve to make decisions that undermined the decisions I had made. It was all very frustrating.

But there was one bright spot – a night auditor by the name of Cheryl who was 21 at the time – ten years my junior. And Cheryl was absolutely beautiful.

I remember the first time I saw her: she had a uniform on and was sitting at her desk, and when I came in, she gave me a big smile and said, "Hello, Mr. Wegner."

That was it. I said, "Hello, how are you?" asked her name and introduced myself, but I was already in love.

Of course, I couldn't tell her that. There was a rule that employees were not supposed to date each other. So the next question was, how was I going to get around that? I finally decided that the best way around it was to ignore it.

After a while of playing those romantic games one plays with the opposite sex, I finally asked her out and she agreed. Because our working hours overlapped, we ended up going to play racquetball in the morning and then going to breakfast. I had coffee and eggs, and Cheryl, who had been up all night, had a hamburger and a beer. We had a great time.

It took us a while, but we eventually had a second date, this time over dinner. And here's what I said to her on our second date: "You know, I think we should get married." She thought that was hysterically funny, but she didn't realize what a big thing it was for me since I still had the guilt of being divorced with two children.

That date went well and we started having a relationship. Eventually I met her parents, and let's just say they were underwhelmed with me. Some time later, I met them again and I told them, "You know, Cheryl and I have been talking about getting married and moving to New Jersey, and I think that's what we're going to do."

Neither of us expected her father's reaction. He stood straight up out of his chair, got right in my face and said, "Over my dead body!"

Do you ever look back and realize that God reached out and held your tongue when you were about to say something really bad? I think he did it at that moment because I almost said to Doug, "You know, where I come from, that can be arranged!"

Instead, Doug pulled me to another room and started grilling me about our relationship. Essentially, he didn't much like me, and if I were he, I wouldn't have liked me, either. After all, here was this unknown man ten years older than his daughter taking her away from her parents. But that didn't faze me and what I basically ended up saying to him was, "Doug, I care about your daughter and I don't really care what you say."

And neither did Cheryl.

In just a short time, she announced that she was moving to New Jersey. My time in Boston was up and I was being transferred back. She packed up what possessions she had in her Chevy Vega and moved to the

Garden State. We wanted to get married and we didn't care what her parents thought – or what God thought, either.

Our wedding was in a park chapel with some minister from some unknown denomination that some friend of a friend of a friend had recommended. The reception was in a restaurant in the midst of other diners.

Because we were in the hotel business, we were able to go to San Francisco for our honeymoon. But it wasn't romantic. I wanted to relax, hang around, take it easy. Not Cheryl – she wanted to go out and see and do everything.

That was just the beginning of our conflicts. We argued and fought over everything, even brands of groceries like mayonnaise and ketchup. It could have been really ugly – one of those quick marriages that end in divorce in three months.

But God is merciful even when we're not looking for that mercy. I realized two things: first, that I loved Cheryl, and second, that I wasn't about to become a two-time loser. So I resolved to be more flexible, which is very difficult for a control freak like me.

The other thing going for us was that Cheryl loved me. In other words, despite the quickness with which it happened, we had a true affection, a true love for each other that strengthened our resolve to make it work. We knew it wasn't perfect, and we knew there would be times when we wanted to strangle each other and even times when we would say, "I wonder if this was a mistake." But we were bound and determined in our hearts not to let it fail.

At this point, we didn't acknowledge God, but he knew and loved us. He mercifully honored our determination and began leading us step-by-step back to the fullness of truth.

How? Well, every now and then, we'd go to church. One month it'd be an Episcopalian church, the next month Catholic, then maybe a Pentecostal or Evangelical church. After a few months of this, I said to Cheryl, "You know, I'm at a point in my life where I haven't gone to church for a long time and I'm not sure about my relationship with God. But I think that if we're going to go to any church at all, no matter how often, it's going to have to be a Catholic church, because I just don't feel comfortable anywhere else. It doesn't feel like home."

Cheryl seemed to understand this. She had been baptized Catholic, but raised in a Protestant denomination, while her mother had been Catholic most of her life.

So we started to look at parishes around us. There wasn't any great commitment on my part. It was more like, "I'll go if I feel like it." What I did have a great commitment to was making money.

Chapter 7

The search for mammon

After we got married, the management of the hotel in New Jersey changed hands and I was dumped. So I got a job in a different hotel. Two years later, the ownership there changed and I was fired again. This one was really frustrating. The staff and I had taken this place that was losing hundreds of thousands of dollars a year, remodeled it, given the guests good service and had actually turned a profit.

That didn't matter to the new company, though. One of the partners had a nephew who had just graduated from college and needed a job. So they gave him mine.

It came as a complete shock to me. I had no idea this was coming and when the corporate guy told me this was going to happen, I didn't know what to do – jump on him, cry, spit or what.

I had an hour-long commute and I pondered and fretted all the way home about what I was going to do next. And this thought came to me: "You know, isn't that just the way it is with these high-powered money guys?" They didn't care about people like me or others who were trying to make a living. The more I turned it over in my mind, the more I resented them, the idea of working for them, and even the idea of working for anyone at all.

By the time I got home, I made this pledge out loud: "I'm never *ever* going to work for anybody again!"

Real estate came to my mind because I had acquired a real estate license when I was a teacher and my brother-in-law managed a real estate business. He referred me to another company and I started working as an independent agent for them. There were a few obstacles – I had never owned a house in my life; I didn't know the area I was working since I didn't live there, didn't know anybody there, and hadn't even been there; there was nothing there except farms and a few housing developments; interest rates were at 20% at the time; and no one there had even heard of the company I was doing business with because it was new to the area.

Add to this one other crucial factor – Cheryl became pregnant. And here we were living totally on commission with no income whatsoever.

That, of course, made it a do-or-die situation. So I followed up every lead like a crazy man. God was again merciful. A local builder sent every real estate office in the area a letter saying that a couple of years before when interest rates were even higher, they couldn't sell all the units in some townhouses and adult communities, so they had rented them for a couple of years. Now those leases were coming up and they wanted to sell them off.

I saw this letter and I got a wild idea. I called the builder up and said, "John, I'd like to come over and talk to you about the possibility of you doing business strictly with my real estate company." He agreed, and I got my manager – who was in complete shock – and we went over there.

Now, I'd been in the real estate business for a grand total of six weeks, I'd had no training, and while most real estate offices have twenty or thirty people working in them, ours only had three. But I told John why I thought he should list his properties with me. And he said, "You know, it sounds like a good idea."

"How many do you have?" I asked.

"I have eighty of 'em," he answered, "and I'll give you five at a time."

That was a great way to start in the business and I sold these over the next couple of years.

Cheryl and I still struggled in the beginning because it sometimes takes six months to get your money and we didn't have anything. Family members would sometimes bring us groceries. We had a credit card and I would go to a diner to get food for us since you couldn't charge groceries at that time. And on top of this, Cheryl was starting to have morning sickness with the baby. It was not easy.

After about two years with this company, I decided to go into business with my sister and brother-in-law. What a mistake! All the sayings about not going into business with your relatives turned out to be true here. That lasted about two years, but the ill effects lasted a lot longer and it took years to heal some of those relationships.

I finally decided to go out on my own and I opened up shop down the road. And business started booming. At first I only did commercial real estate, but then I went into residential and started to develop land, build houses and fix up rundown places. The money started to pour in hand over fist and I was making hundreds of thousands of dollars.

Now that I had lots of money, I was *somebody*. I was giving to charities, both political parties, and I even gave money to my employees to help with their finances. I was asked by some of the people in town to consider running for the Board of Education because of my background as a teacher. I won the election and the next year was voted in as the president of the board. I had my own cable TV show and was interviewed in the newspapers all the time. I was a member of every committee you can imagine in town. The people in town knew me. I had arrived! I was a big deal!

I was generous and kind and I was really concerned about other people. But I also had an ulterior motive – I wanted people to like me and, even more, I wanted them to owe me.

And, oh yeah, I was obnoxious about it. Not publicly, of course; but privately I was an idiot.

Even to Cheryl. If Cheryl was complaining and we were having an argument, I'd say, "Well, *you* don't make any money. *You're* not bringing anything into the family financially."

Yes, I said that to her when she was taking care of our two very young children and all the things around the house. If Cheryl were writing this chapter, she would tell you that the times we had money were the most unhappy of her life. While she was at home with two children, I was out *being somebody.* She'd say to me, "Are you going out again tonight?" And I'd say, "Listen, you don't seem to understand this. I go out five or six nights a week, I'm working twelve to fourteen hour days and I'm involved in the community. I'm building our future. I'm giving back to the community. *I'm doing this for you and the children.* Do you think I'm doing this for myself?"

What a jerk I was! Of course, I was doing it for myself! But God used it for my good because while I was out being involved in my community and living the American dream, Cheryl felt so desperate and had such a void to fill that she actually started to hang around with a bunch of *Catholic women!*

She had found a Bible study of four women and they'd pray and read and study the Scriptures. This was the beginning of her conversion process. These women would go to charismatic and evangelization conferences or parish missions together and their numbers started to grow. They started to develop a great little community of about twelve to fifteen women.

We'd socialize with the couples and I thought they were kind of weird. I didn't mind being with them and their husbands. But, of course, I was the best husband there since I made the most money and dressed the best while they were kind of nerdy. Then I would go to socialize with the "real" people – the people with money, power and politics.

Cheryl was starting to go to church and I'd join her on occasion since it was the right thing to do. But as she was growing closer to the Lord, I was growing closer to money.

One day, the two clashed in a dramatic and definitive way. I came home with a check for more than $250,000 that I'd just made on a land deal.

"Look at this!" I said to her. "Look at this!"

And I stuck it right in her face.

"Look at this! Isn't this good? Look at me! Look at me! Look what I did!"

"Oh yeah," she replied. "Mm-hmm."

"Well, what do you think? What do you think? Isn't this good?"

"I'll tell you what I think of this, Bill. I think we should get down on our knees and thank God for that."

Boy, did that get me angry. "Yeah, right, sure, that'll happen. That'll happen. Let me tell you something, sweetie. This was me. This was *my* hard work. This was *my* business skill. This was *my* intelligence. This was my being able to look at a circumstance and say, 'Listen, with some hard work, we can make some money here.' *I* did this."

And then I got right in her face and said: "*God had nothing to do with it.*"

Chapter 8
Messed up and loved

"God had nothing to do with it."

Wow, what arrogance – it makes me shiver just to think I had that kind of attitude. I was seriously messed up.

There's the story of the guy who's out walking in a field and comes upon this large cesspool. In the middle of the cesspool is another guy who is up to his chin in the stuff.

"Hey, how can I help you?" the first guy asks.

"You really want to help me?"

"Yeah, what can I do?"

"Don't make waves!"

In other words, don't mess with my mess, 'cause I like it. And the mess was this – I had no relationship with God at all. I didn't think about him, I didn't pray and when I went to church, I only went through the motions in a cold and mechanical way.

But I've come to know this about God – he loves me not because I'm good, but because *he's* good. Even though I was stuck in my mess and I liked my mess, in his goodness God was not happy to leave me in my mess. So he made waves and in his infinite compassion, he did a wonderful thing – he let me lose all my money.

After I said those awful words to Cheryl, something happened in my life – my arrogance and conceit started to get the best of me. Since I had all the money now, hey, I didn't need any partners or advisors or anyone, no matter how much more experienced than me, to tell me what to do. So, just like when I went into bookmaking, I got to be as stupid as I wanted to be. I'd do some really dumb things with my money, but instead of saying I did something wrong, taking my losses and cutting, I started to throw good money after bad. That started a downward spiral, one that was almost irreversible and one that got me into serious trouble, including some serious debt.

There is one group that is really particular about its money and that's the Federal government. And when you owe the Internal Revenue Service money, they make sure they get to know you. Well I went into debt to the IRS to the tune of $60,000 for one quarter's worth of income tax. They would write me little love notes and leave them at my door, notes like, "We're going to take your house" and, "We're going to close your business."

This was really embarrassing to me because I was a public figure in town. I had my own cable TV show, I had been elected to the Board of Education for a three-year term and two of those years were as president (that was unprecedented; no one had served more than a one-year term as president before), and a small group of people had asked me to consider running for state senate.

So as I started to lose money, I shrank away from the spotlight.

But something more was going on. The money which had defined me for years was now being eaten up by my stupidity and I started to get fearful, panicky, anxious, and above all, depressed. I couldn't think and I wanted to stay in bed all day even though I still had the real estate office. I had no desire to do anything. The office personnel shrank from twenty-five down to four. And on top of my stupidity, the economy turned down again and people stopped buying houses.

Then, of course, the IRS was rather unrelenting in the pursuit of their money. My mailbox became my enemy. I would literally stand at the end of my driveway staring at it for two or three minutes before I had the courage to open it up. If there wasn't anything from the IRS, then my day was OK. But if I saw the dreaded words "Internal Revenue Service," I would almost start to hyperventilate.

I tried to function during the day and stop by the office every now and then. I was searching the want ads and I even applied for jobs – me, the big-time business owner, applying for jobs. And I always got the same reply – "Sorry, we can't hire you; you're too qualified."

Nighttime was horrible. I couldn't sleep for more than an hour or two because I had panic attacks where I'd wake up with my heart racing and I was sweating even though the room was cool and the window open. I'd have chest pains and nightmares. I was so fearful that my family was going to lose our home and I was going to be humiliated.

And Cheryl? She knew what was going on, but her faith was in Someone else, not in me. So she was calm, relaxed, peaceful, smiling – and sleeping like a rock. And man that annoyed me. At night when I was out of bed, I'd say out loud to her, "I can't believe you're sleeping like that. I can't believe it! Don't you worry like me? What's the matter with you?" She just kept right on sleeping.

Finally, in the middle of one night I got really desperate. I got up as quietly as I could, went into the bathroom, closed and locked the door and turned on the light. I sat down on the edge of the bathtub and took out Cheryl's Bible.

I started to leaf through the pages. "There's got to be something in here," I told myself. "She reads this thing all the time and she's sleeping like a baby and I'm not – I'm sitting in the bathtub."

Then, for the first time in my life, I prayed. When I was young, I had *said* prayers, but now I *prayed*. I prayed because I had nowhere else to go. Here's what I said out loud to God in my bathroom at about four in the morning. Even in my desperate prayer I was arrogant: "God, if you exist (wow, what a way to start) – if any of the stuff they've been saying about you is true – you need to help me. I've come to this conclusion, Lord: I'm not in charge and I really need you to help me.

"God, if you're there – if you are for real – will you help me? I don't have anywhere else to go. I know that I'm not in charge of this thing. And I think I'm just going to explode and die unless you help me."

And you know what happened? No one appeared in my bathroom. No flash of light. No smell of flowers. But he did help me. I was able to go back to bed and sleep for a few hours. A miracle.

I think the story of the Prodigal Son should really be named the story of the Loving Father (Luke 15:11-32). You know the story already of the younger of two sons who tells his father, "You're as good as dead already, Pops, so give me my share of the inheritance." He goes off to another country and begins to spend his money wildly on parties and women and making friends. And then he runs out of money. He has no one to turn to and ends up on the lowest end of things for a Jewish boy – feeding pigs. It's so bad he can't even eat the corncobs he's giving the pigs. One day, he says to himself, "This is desperate, I'm starving to death, I'm feeding pigs, I smell bad and I look disgusting. What's the worst that can happen to me if I go home? I can go and beg my father to make me a slave since even they live better than I do."

Meanwhile, the father is going out everyday to look for his son's return. Everyday he goes out and waits to see if he'll come home.

Finally, one day the father sees a speck on the horizon. You know that you can pick your kids out anywhere, even in a crowd. The father sees it and he knows instantly it's his son and that son is coming home. And this wealthy man picks up his robes and runs, *runs*, to meet his son. Do we get that? He runs.

If one of our children did that, most likely we'd be saying something like, "Wait till that sucker gets here. He'd better come home with his tail between his legs, 'cause something's going to change in this house. I told him once and I'll tell him again, it's either my way or...."

But that's not how it is with God. He has a goofy kind of love that doesn't make any sense. He is crazy about us. If God the Father had a refrigerator, our picture would be on it. We are his beloved. All I had to do was *turn* towards God and he came running after me.

My real estate business started to get busy and prosper. My own people would call me and say, "Bill, what's going on? How come we're so busy?" And I'd say, "I don't know." It was nothing I did because I was still too depressed to even go to the office.

Things kept getting better and better. I even paid off the IRS. They were so excited I thought they were going to give me a dinner!

To put this in perspective, one day I was driving along with my daughter Kati, who was seven at the time. Kati loves to sing and she's got a beautiful voice. But at that time of her life she didn't care what the real words were – if she didn't know them, she made them up. So she's singing the hymn "Abba, Father" and that should go like this:

Abba,
  Abba, Father,
Mold us,
  Mold us and fashion us...

But here's what I heard Kati singing:

Abba,
  Abba, Father,
Roll us,
  Roll us and flatten us...

Of course I laughed. But then it hit me – that's what happened to me! God permitted me to get rolled and flattened so I could turn to him when there was nowhere else to go.

God's answer to my prayer was overwhelming. My businesses started to get back into shape and so did my marriage. You see while I was struggling with the loss of my money, Cheryl had been making inquiries into the Catholic faith and she started going through the Rite of Christian Initiation of Adults so she could be confirmed and receive the Eucharist. In order for her to complete that, her marriage to me had to be valid in the eyes of the Church, and at the time it wasn't. Remember, I had been divorced and had two children from that previous marriage. When Cheryl and I got married, we didn't even bother going to the Catholic Church about it.

So as far as the Church was concerned, we were living in sin – and the Church was right! After all, Jesus did say, "Every one who divorces his wife and marries another commits adultery, and he who marries a woman divorced from her husband commits adultery." (Lk 16:18)

A nun who was in Cheryl's Bible study and who was leading her through the RCIA told her that I needed to apply for an annulment. I did it, but without any real willingness. It was granted and we had our marriage validated in the Catholic Church.

So my marriage was now on solid footing and my businesses were getting back there, too. I was thinking, "This is good. I like this; I'm back, I'm on a roll."

I had a business attitude towards God. He had done something for me and now the right thing would be to do something for him. Now, I thought what is the least I can do for God? Well, I could go back to church and receive the sacraments. God would like that. So I went to Confession for the first time in 25 years. That was interesting. I told that poor priest everything. At the end of my one-hour plus confession he said in a wobbly voice "Well, welcome back." So here I was a Sunday Catholic giving God my 60 minutes each week and living my life the way I wanted to the rest of the time. But that was about to change.

Cheryl and her women's Bible-study group had started to attend conferences and workshops to learn more about their faith. I wanted nothing to do with that!

But one time I wanted to take a weekend trip with Cheryl to the Bahamas. We owned a travel agency and that was a perk we received from a tour company. Well, Cheryl pulled the "Let's Make a Deal" thing on me. She only agreed to the trip if I would go with her, Erin, Kati and another family to a conference in South Jersey. I said yes thinking that when the time came I would wiggle my way out of it.

But Cheryl wasn't hearing any of that. I told her I would rather have a root canal than go there, but she didn't seem to care. So off we went.

We missed all of Friday night because of my procrastination. Saturday morning we showed up – late, of course, because of me – at this big convention center. I looked in and there were 2500 way-too-happy-for-me people. Also, there were no seats available. So, I thought, this is my way out. I offered to take everyone to breakfast. That went over well with the kids but old eagle-eye Cheryl spied some seats in the first row. How Catholic. So I was quick on my feet and I said, "those seats must be saved". Cheryl saw an usher and told me to go ask him if we could sit there. You guessed it; he said, "Sure those seats are just waiting there for you guys." I almost kicked him.

There we were in the front row and this speaker came out on stage and started talking about how to live as a disciple of Jesus. That we were to show mercy and offer forgiveness. He told us of episodes in his life and how through God's grace he was able to do just that. Well, at first I couldn't stand the guy, but after a while I really started to listen and the Holy Spirit got a hold of me. I realized for the first time in my life that I was not and never had been a follower of Jesus, and you know what? I started to cry. I mean this was a good cry, tears and sobs and everything else. I tried to hide it from my daughters, but they caught on. They, too, started to cry because they thought I missed my Dad who had died recently. Pretty soon my wife saw the three of us crying away and she started crying with us. Before long the other family joined in and we now had the whole row crying and I was the only one who knew why!

On the ride home the next day I told Cheryl that I was going to get serious about my faith. I was no longer going to be just a Sunday Catholic. I was going to read, study and live my faith the best I could. But I was still going to spend time making money and doing the things in life I loved, like golf and such.

And then God started to whisper to me. Quietly at first. Have you ever felt when God was calling you that you could just let the answering machine take a message? I felt like saying, "Not now, Lord! Not now! I'm on a roll here! I'm coming back! Leave a message and I'll get back to you."

But he was persistent with his whispering. And he kept saying, "Why don't you come work for me?"

God's got a great sense of humor and he's full of surprises. Here's a guy who worshiped money his whole adult life, who did some stupid things to get it and God makes him a full-time evangelist in a ministry that doesn't charge anything for what it does. That hurts!

But God put people in my life who were working for him who'd had successful careers before – lawyers, brokers, and financial managers. They encouraged me and through various ways, Cheryl and I were able to get rid of the businesses and simplify our lives so I could go out and proclaim God's word to everyone.

Chapter 9

Reconciliation hurts

When God calls someone to ministry, he's not only thinking about the people that person is going to reach, but above all he always has that person's salvation in mind. The same is true for me. When he called me to ministry, I gave everything up to follow that call. The call to ministry, of course, doesn't make me or anyone else holy. Just like everyone else, we have to "work out our salvation in fear and trembling," as St. Paul says. So in his mercy, God puts things in my life to help me to become holy.

Have you ever noticed that the Scriptures are full of sinners? Moses murdered an Egyptian. David committed adultery with Bathsheba. Peter denied Jesus during the Passion. Now there are other murderers and adulterers and cowards in the Bible as well, but we don't go naming our children after them. There's Judas, Herod and Jezebel, to name a few. What's the difference, then, between Moses, David and Peter and the other three? The difference is reconciliation. Moses, David and Peter were reconciled with God, while Judas, Herod and Jezebel, well we don't know if they were reconciled or not. That is why we will name our sons David or Peter, but not Judas or Herod.

When Jesus gave his sermon on the plain in Luke's Gospel (6:12-49), the first thing he said after he gave the beatitudes was this: "But I say to you that hear, love your enemies, do good to those who hate you, bless those who curse you, pray for those who abuse you...If you love those who love you, what credit is that to you? For even sinners love those who love them. And if you do good to those who do good to you, what credit is that to you? For even sinners do the same...But love your enemies, and do good...and your reward will be great and you will be sons of the Most High, for he is kind to the ungrateful and the selfish. Be merciful, even as your Father is merciful." (6:27-28, 32-33, 35-36)

One of the blessings I had in ministry was to be invited to Northern Ireland to speak to about three to four hundred Catholics and Protestants who were gathered at the Protestant Cathedral of St. Anne's in Belfast City, Northern Ireland to pray for healing and peace for their country. It was the night of the vote on the Good Friday Peace Accord in May of 1998.

I was able to tell those Protestants and Catholics that they needed to love their enemies and return good for evil. As if they didn't know that. That's nothing new, of course; I was only repeating what Jesus had told us. But I brought that message to people who were part of a society engaged in a fratricidal conflict – brother killing brother – and constantly at odds with each other over the faith, of all things.

As I found out later, those words of Jesus are easy to say and a lot harder to live. It's especially easy if you don't have serious enemies. And, even though I had been in both business and politics, I didn't have any really major enemies.

But God loves me so much that he gave me a big enemy, so I could practice my faith and grow in holiness.

Michael (not his real) was one of the reasons I got into full-time ministry in the first place. I loved this man. He was a real mentor and even a father figure to me. He's an older man and my family loved him also, and even though he lived in another part of the country, he would come to visit us regularly. He was always welcome. There was a true friendship there. Or so I thought.

One night, when I was out on a local parish mission, Michael was visiting my house. Get the picture – I'm gone from my house, and a trusted friend is visiting. And this trusted friend made sexual advances towards my wife. How would you respond?

Now as you may have already figured out, I have a wonderful wife. Next to God, Cheryl knows me the best. And she knew this about me – that even though I can go around the world and preach to people to love their enemies and to return good for evil, she knew I had not changed very much. You see Cheryl knew my act back then. She knew me as the guy who, if you cut him off in the parking, lot would follow you *into* Sears and ask you where you got your driver's license. So she was wise enough to wait until Michael was long gone before she told me about this.

And when she did, I was in a kind of shock. I started to laugh. "Oh, come on, you're kidding me." But she wasn't kidding me. I think I even said something really ridiculous like, "Are you sure you didn't misinterpret this?" As if a woman could possibly do that in this circumstance.

I didn't know what to do, where to turn, where to look or who to talk to. It took me a while to realize that I was pretty angry. But I wasn't angry with this guy or Cheryl or even myself. The anger with Michael would come later.

At first I was only angry with God.

I felt that God had tricked me, that he did me dirty. So I entered into a "conversation" with God. "I cannot believe you would let this happen to me, God. I've given up everything for you." Yes, I gave God the "after all I did for you" talk.

In fact, this was kind of how I felt after leaving my worldly wealth behind. I had owned five businesses, I had a vacation house in Disney World in Florida as well as a beautiful house in New Jersey, I had the latest cars and clothes, took great vacations, gave money to the Republicans, the Democrats, the Independents – anyone who asked for money. I used to have a cable TV show called, "Real Estate Review with Bill Wegner." After my conversion, instead of interviewing builders and lawyers and real estate agents on the show, I started inviting priests and nuns and Catholic lay evangelists. Mine was a very public conversion. And people started talking about me. "That Bill Wegner has really lost it. He's gone off the deep end. He's a Jesus freak now; he only wants to talk about God."

One day, a friend of mine, a guy who at one time had sold mortgages in my real estate office, was coming out of the grocery store as I was going in. It was a cold day and Carl was dressed this way: he had on a New York Rangers jacket, a New Jersey Devils sweatshirt, New York Knicks sweatpants, a New York Giants hat and New York Jets wrist bands. Now picture that.

"Hi, Carl," I said, "how are you doing?"

"Oh, Bill, how are *you* doing? I heard about you. I heard that you really went a little crazy. That you're a fanatic."

And I looked at Carl dressed up in all his sports paraphernalia and said, "Yea, Carl, one of us is."

I can sometimes feel like Jeremiah, the prophet: "I have become a laughingstock all day long; everyone mocks me." (Jer. 20:7)

In a way, though, that kind of ridicule is easier to deal with than betrayal. Jesus tells us clearly that when we follow him it will not be easy. His command to "Take up your cross daily and follow me" is fair warning that life with him is going to be rough.

But this kind of betrayal was beyond what I was expecting. A man I trusted to do the right thing was making passes at my wife – and God let it happen. "I cannot believe you would let that happen. People think I'm an idiot already. They think I'm nuts. No wonder you can't get anyone to work for you."

I was so angry. I started to turn my anger and hatred toward Michael. It was so bad that I started thinking about taking revenge on him. Then I started to hear more stories about what he'd done with other women. And every time I got a new bit of information, I would hate him even more.

I was beginning to realize that I was acting as I had been acting before my conversion. In fact, there was a little voice inside of me saying something to me – "Bill, you're not supposed to act that way. You're supposed to be a follower of Jesus Christ. You're not supposed to hate; you're not supposed to seek revenge."

But I said to that voice, "Shut up. I can't deal with you now."

Yet I couldn't do anything else. I certainly couldn't pray. Everything that happened to me at that time was filtered through this experience. This guy was my sole thought. I was only talking to people who would talk with me about him and what he had done. That's what I talked about most with my wife and with my co-workers in the ministry. I was obsessed with him. I definitely couldn't pray for him because I couldn't think anything good or pray anything good about him.

Over time, something started to happen. Here is how God worked in all of this. I became desperate because I was full of hatred, revenge, fear and anger. I was living in my own private self-made hell and I didn't like it. So I started seeking more counsel from my spiritual director. And when I talked to him and others, they'd say, "Hey, Bill. Can we pray?" or "There's a Scripture verse I'd like you to look at." Then someone I knew, who had heard what was going on would say, "Bill, I was at my Bible study last night and we were studying Scripture and I thought of you when we read this particular scripture." And it was the same verse my spiritual director mentioned to me. It was Luke 7:36-50. As thickheaded as I was, when three or four people mentioned the same Bible passage in the course of a few days, even I took notice.

I read that passage some fifty to sixty times. This is the story of when Jesus was invited by Simon the Pharisee to have supper with him. Jesus went to Simon's house and a woman, "a sinful women from the city" – in other words, a prostitute – came in and went right up to Jesus, knelt at his feet and started to cry. Now, we've all cried before, but I'm not sure that many of us have cried the way she cried that night. Her tears were enough to start cleaning off all the dirt and dust from Jesus' feet. She then kissed them, dried them with her hair and anointed them with a very expensive ointment.

Seeing this, Simon thought Jesus wasn't so great anymore because "if he was a prophet, he would know what kind of woman that was who is touching him – that she is a sinner."

But Simon didn't realize the drawback of inviting Jesus to his house for dinner – that Jesus would know what he was thinking. So when Jesus told him, "Simon, I have something to say to you," and the Pharisee answered, "Yes, Rabbi, what is it?" he had no idea what he was in for. (Actually, Simon reminds me of Eddie Haskell from "Leave it to Beaver." He was a phony just as Eddie was when he would say in that nasally voice of his something like, "Gee, Mrs. Cleaver. That's a lovely dress you're wearing tonight.")

So Jesus tells Eddie, er, I mean Simon, a story about a moneylender who lent some money to two guys. One borrowed $50, the other $500. Neither one could repay the money, so the moneylender forgave them both their debts. Then Jesus asked this question: "Who do you think loves the moneylender the most? The guy who is forgiven $50 or the guy who is forgiven $500?"

Simon is no dummy and answers, "I guess the one who owed the most money." And Jesus answered him, "You have judged rightly."

Then Jesus goes on to list what the woman did for him and what Simon failed to do for him in showing hospitality. When Simon failed to kiss Jesus, wash and dry his feet or anoint his head with oil, he failed to show the most basic hospitality one Jew showed to another at that time. This would be equivalent to my inviting guests to my house and not opening the door for them, not taking their coats or offering them refreshments.

So what Simon failed to do for Jesus, this woman did for him and she did it because "her many sins have been forgiven, so she can show great love."

This is an extraordinary woman. A woman on a mission. She was bound and determined to see this Jesus and she was not going to let anything get in her way. She did not care that Jesus happened to be at a dinner party at the home of a Pharisee. Nor did she care what the people at that dinner might think of her, a prostitute coming into the house of a religious leader and making a spectacle of herself. What was this woman doing by her actions? She was experiencing the Sacrament of Reconciliation. She came to the Master to repent, to confess her sins and receive his forgiveness.

Then Jesus said to Simon, "But he who is forgiven little, loves little."

If you had asked Simon, "Are you a sinner?" he would probably have said something like, "Yes I'm a sinner – but not like her. She's a big-time sinner." Many of us think the same thing. We compare ourselves to others, maybe the Saddams or the Bin Ladens of the world and we might say, "I don't understand why we're all lumped together in this salvation thing. I'm not as big a sinner as some people in the world. I never murdered anyone."

But Jesus tells us, "You have heard that it was said to the men of old, 'You shall not kill; and whoever kills shall be liable to judgment.' But I say to you that every one who is angry with his brother shall be liable to judgment; whoever insults his brother shall be liable to the council, and whoever says, 'You fool' shall be liable to the hell of fire." (Matt. 5:21-22)

I guess, then, that you're reading a book written by a murderer because I hated this guy who hurt not only me but also my family. As I started to read that Scripture over and over again, I started to ask what God was calling me to do and I came to this realization – God was calling me to go and see Michael and forgive him.

As you can imagine, I did not like that idea at all and I struggled with that idea for weeks on end. During my prayer, I would pace back and forth thinking, "What do you want me to do, God?" hoping he would give me another answer.

I was kind of like the atheist who was skiing and fell off a cliff. On his way down, he grabbed a branch and stopped himself, but he was still hundreds of feet away from where he fell and from the bottom. So he started yelling, "Is there anybody up there?" and no one answered. He called again, and still no one answered. Then he yelled as loudly as he could and all of a sudden he heard a voice say, "I'm here."

"Who said that?"

"I did."

"Who are you?"

"God."

"Really?"

"Do you believe?" God asked.

"Of course I believe," the atheist answered.

"Do you really believe?"

"Yes, yes, I really believe."

"All right," God said, "then let go of the branch."

There was a long pause and then the atheist said, "Is there anybody else up there?"

I was like him trying to find something I would agree with. But I kept praying, going to spiritual direction and talking with people about this. And God kept saying to me, "Look at yourself," that is, look at my life and my sins.

So I came to the realization one day that God was not asking me to go to this guy to forgive him. What a relief! God did not want me to forgive Michael.

No – it was worse. The Lord was placing this on my heart: "Bill, you know what your sin is; you worry about you. You concern yourself with you and I'll take care of Michael."

That was fair enough – until God also gave me this on my heart: "Bill, you need to go see this guy, but when you see him, you need to ask him to forgive you." What? "That's right. Ask him to forgive you for hating him, for wanting to kill him, for everything bad you thought and said about him, for all your planned revenge against him. You need to go to see Michael and ask him to forgive you."

I could not believe it. Here one of my best friends had made advances towards my wife and God is telling me to ask him for forgiveness! Here was my response to God: "This must come from you. Only you would think of this! No rational person would think of this. That's never going to happen. I am not going to go ask this guy to forgive me – I didn't do anything. As a matter of fact, that's where that expression 'a cold day in hell' comes from."

But when the Holy Spirit starts working on someone, he doesn't let go and one day about two weeks later I found myself on an airplane heading out to meet

Michael. The reason I did it was pretty selfish. It wasn't because of any great love for him or God. It was simply that I had to do something because I didn't like being in hell anymore.

So I went where I knew he would be speaking and there he was walking towards me. Then we were standing face to face. He just looked at me and didn't say a word. Now I had not seen him or spoken a word to him since the day he left my house months before. But even there, as we're looking at each other, my mind was rebelling. "What are you doing?" I asked myself. "Don't you know what you want to do to him?"

By God's grace only, here's what I said to him: "I just want you to know that I came here today to ask you to forgive me. I would like you to forgive me for all the hatred I had for you in my heart; for all the revenge I had plotted against you; for all the things I fantasized I was going to do to you and to your family and how I was going to get back at you for what you did; for all the fear I had (I was afraid I was going to bump into Michael by accident, maybe in an airport); for everything in my heart that I had against you. If you can find it in your heart to forgive me, that would be a great blessing to me. And if there's any way I can help you or your family, that would be a great blessing to me. And maybe someday we might be able to be reconciled and be friends again."

When I said that, a tremendous miracle took place. All of my burden about this was instantly lifted from me. It was as if God reached down and took a tremendous boulder off of me and *I was free!* I was free from all the pain, all the suffering, all the anger, all the hatred, all the revenge. And I instantly realized something – forgiving this man and asking forgiveness from him wasn't about him deserving it, which he didn't. That act of forgiveness and asking for it was for me. God gave *me* that gift. I learned that when I follow God's command and pay attention to what he tells me to do rather than paying attention to what I think someone *else* is supposed to do, I am freed to obey God and be in a right relationship with him and others, and that brings tremendous peace.

Did Michael benefit from it? Yes, he did. He eventually got help. We in the ministry helped him to seek the right people to help him with his sickness. We talk to each other now, though our friendship is not what it used to be. It might return there, it might not, though I am open to that possibility.

If you want to experience more of God today, here's my advice: find yourself an enemy and extend to that person kindness, mercy and forgiveness under two circumstances: 1) he or she doesn't deserve it (because *we* don't deserve it when God gives it to us), and 2) when you don't feel like it. If we can do that, I guarantee

that the Holy Spirit will show up because we can't do it
without him.

Chapter 10
Loving the Poor

I want to explore something about Jesus that perhaps we take for granted or never even think about or acknowledge. As I've read through the Gospels, I've come to the realization that in Jesus' day, he was the most popular person in the Jewish world.

He was kind of like a movie star. He had people all over him and the apostles were at times protecting him, like bodyguards. Remember when they tried to chase away the mothers who were bringing their children to him? Jesus even had to run away from the crowds at times to be alone and to pray to his Father. One time he fled because they wanted to crown him as king because they had had their fill of bread (Jn. 6:15).

When I started thinking about this, it struck me that we have always treated certain people like this and still do. Even my 80-year-old mother, Mary Rose Lynch Wegner, used to get dressed up as a bobby-soxer when she was a young teenager and go with her friends on the bus to the movie theaters in downtown Newark. They'd go to see these popular singers, the crooners, as they called them, like Frank Sinatra and Dean Martin.

I'd ask her what they did, and she said, "We went down there and we acted like idiots. We would just be screaming, 'Frankie,' and people would be fainting. And when he came out, with the orchestra playing and only the microphone out there, we just went nuts."

It's really hard for me to imagine my Mom acting like that because it seems so undignified. So unmotherly like.

But, of course, when I was a teenager, the Beatles came over to the US and we acted like idiots for them. I can remember being in my room, playing records really loudly and locking the door so no one could come in. The hairbrush was the microphone.

I live right next to Freehold, New Jersey, which is where Bruce Springsteen grew up and went to Catholic school. So I hear this kind of thing: "My brother-in-law's wife's sister's nephew-in-law cuts Bruce's lawn."

"Oh," comes the response, "so you must be pretty close to him yourself."

We always want to be around popular well-known people. We always want to be involved in some way, shape or form, with someone who is a celebrity.

Well, it wasn't that different in Jesus' day and he was popular. Even the apostles were so caught up in the physical realities and in the world's notion of popularity that they used to argue with each other about who was the best apostle.

"I'm number one," one might say.

"No, no, I think you're about number six," another might reply.

Of course, Jesus had to teach them that wasn't what he was about at all, and if they were going to be his disciples, they couldn't be like that, either.

Imagine this – there were about 20,000 people whom he fed with the five loaves and two fish, counting the women and the children. And they sat and listened to him all day long without eating, since they hadn't brought enough food with them. It's almost impossible to visualize something like that happening today. That's enough people to fill a stadium for a basketball game or a rock concert, and you know that no one goes through those without eating. So you know that his preaching must have been something out of the ordinary for them to be able to do that.

Now there are two questions that need to be asked here: 1) Why was Jesus so popular? and 2) Did he *want* to be popular?

So why did all those folks 2,000 years ago want to be with Jesus? Think about it – if Jesus were here today doing what he did back then, wouldn't we want to follow him? Wouldn't we want to see him? I think we would.

Why? Because he was performing miracles. Wouldn't that be a big show? Wouldn't you want to go see someone who had raised his friend from the dead? Wouldn't you want to go see someone who had walked on water and scared the living daylights out of his friends because they thought he was a ghost? If you had heart disease, or cancer or any other serious illness, wouldn't you want to go see someone who could touch and heal you?

Remember the story of the woman with the hemorrhage (Mk. 5:24-34, Lk 8:43-48)? All the apostles are around Jesus, with hundreds of people pressing in on him, and this woman, who has been hemorrhaging for years, wants to get near him. Now she's one determined lady. She fights the crowd that is around Jesus saying to herself, "If only I can just touch his cloak, I will get well." And she does it. When she does, Jesus stops and asks, "Who touched me?"

Now Jesus has his entourage around him, all of the apostles. And when he asks that question, they're saying, "Are you kidding me? About 500 people just touched you."

But Jesus insists, "Who touched me? I felt the power go out of me." And the woman was cured instantly. That, obviously, got around.

Jesus wanted all these crowds around him, but not just to be popular. He didn't want to be popular like movie stars who pretend they want their privacy but then go everywhere the photographers are because if you're not filmed or your picture's not in the paper, then you're nobody.

Jesus wanted the crowds around him because he wanted to preach the Gospel to that crowd. He wanted to tell the people, "I have a new plan for your life" and to show them the glory of God. What better way than to be a miracle worker?

Because of his popularity, there were a lot of people who wanted him in their group. Even the Pharisees, Sadducees and Zionists wanted him in their groups, if they could just convince him of what they thought was the truth of their position. But he did not go to those groups.

Instead, he went to those who were the least popular, those had been thrown out of the synagogue. Jesus called them the lost sheep of the house of Israel. These are the people who were on the outskirts of society. They were called the poor, but they weren't necessarily the poor in the sense of poverty because there were some rich people who were part of "the poor."

Who were the members of the poor? The blind, the lame, the lepers, the deaf, the mentally ill, the shepherds. These were the people who would not or could not keep the Jewish laws.

Who were the first people to find out about Jesus' birth? The shepherds. Why were they part of the poor? Because they couldn't keep the ritual purity laws. They were out taking care of the sheep in the fields and couldn't get to water regularly. So there were shepherds in this group.

Who was the first person to see Jesus after his resurrection? Mary Magdalene. There were prostitutes in this group.

Who were the most hated people of the time? The wealthy tax collectors. Wouldn't you be upset if one of your fellow Americans was collecting taxes for an occupying country? But one of the apostles, Matthew, was a tax collector.

All of these people had been thrown out of the synagogue and the Temple. To us, that may not seem like a big deal because if we are excluded from one church, we can go down the road to another. But it wasn't that way then. If you were thrown out, even your family didn't want to be with you.

Nobody wanted to be in the *anawim*, the little ones, as the Old Testament calls them, and the reason is that they were told, in essence, "God doesn't love you." And everybody in that day believed that, even the apostles. Remember the story in St. John's Gospel (9:1-41) of the man born blind? What was the apostles' question to Jesus? "Rabbi, was it this man's sins or the sin of his parents that caused him to be born blind?"

The thinking was that if you were blind, then you were a sinner and God got you. If you were deaf or you were lame, then God must have got you. And if you were born blind or lame or deaf, then it must have been your parents or grandparents who sinned.

So the poor were excluded from everyone else and no one who was ritually clean was allowed to be with the poor.

But along came Jesus and he said he was going to go after the lost sheep of the house of Israel. He knew he had been anointed by God to preach the good news to the poor. And the good news to them was, "God loves you very much. In fact, he loves you just as much as he loves the chief priest in the Temple." Jesus even said that tax collectors and prostitutes were going to get into heaven before the Pharisees and Sadducees.

So it's easy to see why these people loved him and why he was so popular. It's also easy to see why he was targeted for death. "If you won't be part of us, then we will hate you and have to get rid of you," might have been their thinking.

Jesus said, "The poor you will always have with you." Is that group here today? Is there any group that is excluded from society with whom we – good, holy Catholics that we are – don't want to hang around? Yes, there are. The blind, the handicapped, prostitutes, alcoholics, drug dealers, convicts, people with AIDS, the homeless. You get the picture.

What was Jesus' mandate from his Father? To preach the good news to the poor. What are we supposed to do as his disciples? Preach the good news to the poor. So are we supposed to be hanging out with the poor? Yes we are.

Jesus always brings it down to our level and he points out those who are excluded. But let me ask something here: Have you ever been excluded? I would answer yes, that everybody has been in that excluded group at one time or another. You can be in that group because you're a woman. You can be in that group because you're a man. You can be in that group because you're old. You can be in that group because you're not old enough. You can be in that group because your skin is dark. You can be in that group because your skin is white. You can be in that group because you're too poor or too rich or because you're from the wrong or right side of the tracks or because you can't play kickball right.

I had a tremendous experience with this a couple of years ago in two very different places – North Dakota and Queens, New York. Now, I'm a white, middle aged guy, so I'm not used to being in the minority.

I did a parish mission in a small town in North Dakota one October. When I got there, though, I felt a slight bit excluded, even though it was a great parish with wonderful saints. The reason? Because I'm from out East, and I'm not a farmer. Every single person in that parish had been or currently was a farmer, including the priest. Not me. I didn't know what they were talking about most of the time. We would start having a normal conversation in a group, eventually the talk would turn to farming and I would be thinking to myself, "What language is that?"

The following week I went to Queens, which, of course, is as East as you can get, and definitely not farming country. But there I was the only white guy, not just in the church, but also in the whole neighborhood. Now that is an interesting feeling. What was really funny was when I went up to a little old lady of the parish and asked her if it was OK for me to walk in the neighborhood. "Honey, if you're a white guy around here," she said, "you're either a cop or a priest. No one's going to bother you." And she was right; no one did.

During the 30s and 40s, that Queens parish was the "white" church. Which meant it was only for whites, and the blacks couldn't attend. That, of course, was totally unfair, but that's how it was. So the African-Americans built their own church just down the street from the "white" church. So, the "black" church and the "white" church coexisted within sight of each other. Eventually, the neighborhood changed. All the whites moved out and more blacks moved into the area, and eventually there were only blacks attending the formerly all white church. So now there are two Catholic churches in the neighborhood both attended by black folks and guess what? They don't go to each other's churches! The folks that had been excluded now do the excluding themselves. How does God put up with us?

We don't like to be excluded; we don't like to be different. If you ask Catholic school kids about their uniforms, they'll probably say they hate to wear them. But ask them, as I have, what they wear when they go to the malls on the weekends.

"We wear jeans" How many wear jeans? They all raise their hands.

"We wear T-shirts." Oh really, how many of you wear T-shirts? They all raise their hands.

"And sneakers" All hands go up.

"So you all wear uniforms?"

"Oh," they'll say. And a look of awareness comes over their faces.

Look at how the elderly dress. It's certainly different from the kids, but they're wearing essentially the same things every other old person is wearing.

We don't want to be excluded and that has never changed. But Jesus is telling us this: "If you want an opportunity for grace, include the excluded. Love the unlovable."

I have people like that in my family. There's one family member with whom nobody wants to be. The only good thing is that I live in New Jersey and she lives in another state far away.

But the way I deal with her shows me where my selfishness is, where my comfort level is. Every time I'm with her, it's an adventure and most of the time I really don't feel like going on an adventure. "Oh, she's not coming for Christmas?" I'll say in an exaggerated tone. "Oh, bummer."

But every now and then, God pours his grace out on me and I will actually say to my wife, "Ch-Ch-Cheryl?" (am I really saying this out loud?) "Why d-d-d-don't we inv-v-v-v-vite so and so for the weekend?" (God, why did I say that?)

And she'll come to our house and it might be an adventure, but it's also an opportunity for grace and growth.

There are many people in our parishes, our families, our work, our neighborhoods, our schools, who are here for our sanctification, for our salvation, so we can practice our faith. Our faith is in Jesus who died on the cross for us and we believe that he gives us the grace to love others as he loved us – unconditionally. So we should look at them as gifts from God.

If that can happen, then we will have participated in a miracle. Everyone thinks it's a miracle when we pray to God and he does something we've asked him to do. But how about if we look at it the other way around – we pray to God, he pours out his grace, and we do what *he* wants us to do. Now that's also a miracle, isn't it?

God loves us very much and he gives us everything we need to be holy – even people. So find the excluded people, the poor, in your life and spend time with them. If you want to become holy, they're a great source of blessing and a great source of grace.

Chapter 11
Practical consequences of love

"Love your enemies and do good, and lend, expecting nothing in return; and your reward will be great and you will be sons of the Most High; for he is kind to the ungrateful and the selfish. Be merciful even as your Father is merciful."

Luke 6.35-36

Jesus is the supreme teacher. He's our rabbi, which means "teacher" in Hebrew.

(I get to fake out all my Jewish friends by saying, "Well, I was talking to my rabbi the other day..." And they say, "Huh? You converted?" "No, no, no. But I do have a rabbi. His name is Jesus." And then they groan.)

Our rabbi teaches us in so many ways. He teaches us by preaching to us, as in his two Sermons. But more often than not, he teaches us through his encounters with people, like the encounter he had with the sinful woman. He didn't preach anything there, but he certainly taught a tremendous lesson.

Or take the encounters he had with the Scribes and Pharisees. There is a lot for us to learn there from the dialogue he has with them.

He also taught by telling stories – the parables. The lost sheep, the lost coin, the prodigal son.

But what I've discovered (because I'm not that bright – it's been there for 2,000 years and I just found this out) is that one of the most powerful ways Jesus teaches us is by asking direct questions throughout Scripture. He does just what any good teacher would do. "Did you do your homework last night? Well, then, what's the answer to this?"

Throughout the Gospels, there are about 35 or 40 questions that Jesus asks. Some of them are really basic. Like the time he asked Peter, "Simon, son of John, do you love me more than these?"

Or there's the day that he's teaching in a house and someone comes and says to him, "Your mother and your brothers are outside." And here's his response: "Who are my brothers? Who is my mother?"

Remember Cana? That is such a great encounter because it encapsulates the whole mother and child relationship. Mary says to her 30-year-old son, "They're out of wine." And is his response is basically, "So? That seems like somebody else's problem, Mom." Literally it's, "What does that have to do with me?" But does she know her son, or what? She doesn't say another word to him and turns to the other people and says, "Do whatever he tells you." You can almost imagine Jesus saying, "But Mom, my time hasn't come yet. Oh, alright, I'll do it for my Mom."

One day, right at the beginning of his ministry, Jesus was walking by the Jordan River and John the Baptist was there. John tells those around him, "There is the Lamb of God, the one I've been telling you about." That's his mission, of course, to point out to others who Jesus is.

Even though John is pointing him out, his disciples don't know who Jesus is because he has really done nothing public up to this point. Eventually, though, two of John's disciples, John and Andrew, get up and follow Jesus down the road. Jesus turns around and sees them and he asks them a really basic question. It's a question he's not only asking them; it's one he asks us everyday, "What are you looking for?"

If Jesus came into your room right now and asked you that question, what would you say? That's a rather pointed question, isn't it?

When Jesus asks it of John and Andrew, they really don't know how to respond. What do you say to that kind of question? So they answer the question with a question. "Where are you staying?"

That, of course, can seem kind of odd to us. But they're really asking something more profound than that. What they're really saying is, "We want to know more about you." And Jesus answers the question by saying this: "Come and see." He is inviting us to take a look at his three years of ministry.

Looking at those three years, what one word would you use to sum up his ministry? I think it's the word, "love." Loving your neighbors, loving your enemies, loving God.

We need to take a look at that word and how we use it. In the English language, there's only one word for love. So we say, "I love what you've done to your hair" or, "I love pizza" or, "I love my wife." I hope I love my wife more than I love pizza.

In Jesus' day, though, there were four types of love. There's affection, or what the Greeks called *stergos*. It's what we naturally feel for our parents, for instance.

Then there's *eros*, erotic love or romantic love. Remember that guy who's spent the last 30 years sitting on the couch watching TV? You used to be romantically in love with him at one time or another. You can't figure out why now, but you were.

Oh, but it was good when it happened, wasn't it? I remember that when I fell in love with Cheryl, I was living in New Jersey and she was in Massachusetts. I would have walked those 250 miles barefoot over broken glass to go see her.

Of course, after a while those romantic feelings change. If we only operated on our feelings, life would be a never-ending roller coaster.

But our American culture is stuck in a Hollywood-type of love, or what a friend in the ministry, Brian

Casey, calls a hamburger/french fry love. I can identify with that because I love hamburgers and french fries. When you go to nicer restaurant, a place where maybe you pay $7 or $8 for a burger and fries, the server will ask you how you want your burger cooked. (At a fast food place it doesn't matter how you want it cooked. You are getting it "their way.") I would say, "medium rare." But if I really wanted to tell the server how I wanted it, I would have said, "I want mine medium rare. I want it hot and little a pink inside. I don't want it really greasy. I don't want the bun to be soggy, but nice and firm. I want a nice piece of lettuce and a slice of tomato and a little bit of onion. And the fries are going to be medium – not soggy and not burned." And when it comes out, ooooh, it looks good, it smells good and it tastes good.

Well, that's how Hollywood says we're supposed to think of each other. But as time goes by, things start to change – buns get soggy and french fries start to droop. So what's Hollywood's response? They say, "Hey, this isn't what I ordered. Send it back and get me a new one."

Love between a man and a woman starts out as a feeling and that's the way God made us so we would be attracted to each other and we can carry out his first command to us – "Be fruitful and multiply." But it can't stay that way. Eventually it has to turn into a decision.

Somewhere along the line when I was dating Cheryl, we had this discussion: "You know what, honey? There's a new restaurant open in town. Why don't we go there tonight?"

You know what she said? "I don't want to go there."

"Whaaat?"

"I want to go to the movies. There's a movie I'd like to see."

"But I want to go to that restaurant."

OK, so doing both was really obvious, but neither one of us thought of that. Instead, I had a decision to make. She didn't look so attractive that day and I'm sure I didn't look so attractive to her, either. But I made a decision that day to compromise to keep our relationship together, and we continue to make decisions like that everyday in order to love others.

Then there's *philio* love, the filial love we have for our brothers and sisters, our friends and our country.

Finally, there's *agape* love. That's the kind of love Jesus came to model for us. He said we are to love one another as he loves us. And how he loves us is unconditionally; there's nothing we can do to earn this love. Can we do anything that would justify God coming to earth and dying on the cross for us? None of us is worthy enough to earn this. We say at Mass, "Lord, I am not worthy to receive you." Even though we are not worthy, he still does it. Why? Because he loves us.

Of course, he doesn't just love us "good people." He loves "bad people" the same way he loves the "good people." Do you believe that God loves us in the same way he loves Mother Teresa? Do you believe that he loves Mother Teresa in the same way he loves Osama bin Laden? He loves the Holy Father the same as he loves Saddam Hussein. The mass murderer is loved as much as the saint.

"But that's not fair!" you might say.

That's right. God's not about fair, he's about unconditional love.

We might think how wonderful that is and what a nice thought that is, but then there's the second part – "Now you do the same."

"What do you mean, Lord?"

"You do the same."

"I'm supposed to love Osama bin Laden? I can't do that."

"You're right. You can't do that – without me."

Let's look at the progression of civilization. Go back to the caveman days with me for a little bit. My name was Ug and I went out hunting with my spear one day when food was a little scarce and I came across a rabbit. Unbeknownst to me, over on the side of the hill was Uga-muga from another village and he saw the same rabbit. We both threw our spears at the same time, and they both hit it. What happened next? It's pretty easy to predict. We got into a fight, Uga-muga poked my eye out and won. I went back to my village and told the tale and Uga-muga went back to his village and told the tale. But my village was bigger than his. So we decided to take our revenge. We went over there and killed Uga-muga and his family and burned his village to the ground.

That can only go on for so long. If that happened too often, there would only be one village left. So lines of authority developed and laws came into being, like the Code of Hammurabi. But God was revealing better ways to the Israelites. He said, "an eye for an eye." That may seem cruel, but it was actually a way to limit damage.

As time went on, the Silver Rule was developed – "Don't do to others what you would not want them to do to you." And Jesus' Golden Rule, "Do unto others as you would have them do unto you."

Finally, Jesus tops even what he himself said before with this, "Love one another as I have loved you," And "Love your enemies."

In John's Gospel (21:1-19) after the Resurrection, the apostles are out fishing and not catching anything and Jesus tells them to cast their net on the other side. When they do, they catch a whole boatful of fish and Peter then recognizes the Lord.

After they get to shore, Jesus starts talking to Peter saying, "Peter, do you love me more than these?" Jesus asks him that question three times. And Peter responds three times saying, "Lord, you know that I love you."

But here's what Jesus is really saying to him:,"Peter, do you *agape* me?" And here's what Peter answered: "Lord, you know I *philio* you."

So Jesus is asking him, "Do you love me unconditionally so that you'll do anything for me?" And Peter is replying, "I love you like a brother, Lord."

Finally, on the third try, Jesus says, "Peter, son of John, do you *philio* me?" And Peter is hurt, isn't he? But he replies, not with "Lord, you know all things. You know I *agape* you," but with, "you know I *philio* you."

Obviously, he couldn't do what Jesus was asking him to do and neither can we. Even with people we should be loving easily – our spouses, siblings, parents, children – we sometimes withdraw our love from them.

Peter couldn't do it and we can't do it except in one way – living in the power of the Holy Spirit. Remember that it was after Pentecost that Peter was able to suffer for the sake of the Name and rejoice in it (Acts 5:41).

God gives us everything we need to love unconditionally the way he does – expecting nothing in return. It's tough, but he does give us the grace to do it because he loves us.

Chapter 12
Don't miss the point

Someone once sent me this short, five-chapter autobiography:

Chapter 1

I walk down a street. There is a deep hole in the sidewalk. I fall in. I am lost. I am helpless. It isn't my fault. It takes forever to get out.

Chapter 2

I walk down the same street. There is a deep hole in the sidewalk. I pretend I don't see it. I fall in again. I can't believe I'm in the same place. But it isn't my fault. It takes a long time to get out.

Chapter 3

I walk down the same street. There is a deep hole in the sidewalk. I see it is there. I still fall in. It's a habit. I know where I am. It is my fault. I get out immediately.

Chapter 4

I walk down the same street. There is a deep hole in the sidewalk. I walk around it.

Chapter 5

I walk down a different street.

Aaaaah! Conversion.

I think a lot of us are like this. We tend to follow the definition of insanity – doing the same thing over and over again and expecting a different result. But when we get to following Jesus, he can interrupt that cycle and lead us down a different street.

When I had my conversion experience and came back to the Church, I decided that I was going to follow Jesus down that different street. And for the first time in my life, I really heard what the Lord Jesus wants us to do in following him – love our enemies, return good for evil, bless those who curse us, do good to those who hate us, give to all without expecting repayment, get rid of all of our "stuff" (it's all in the Sermon on the Mount and the Sermon on the Plain). I realized that I had spent my whole life doing the opposite of what Jesus wants us to do. It was a point of conversion for me, what I like to call a John the Baptist moment, a moment when someone points out Jesus to us.

St. John the Baptist is one of my favorite people in all of the Scriptures. At the time he came, there was such an anticipation for the Messiah to come that they had the Messiah *de jour*.

"Look, is he the one?"

"No, no."

"Maybe that's him over there."

"Ah, I guess not."

John the Baptist's ministry caused a lot of excitement among the people, so much excitement that even soldiers were coming to be baptized. And the reason for that was simple – he told it the way it was. He didn't pull any punches with anyone, which is also why he lost his head.

Of course too much is excitement is going to get noticed by the religious authorities – and it did. One day a delegation appears to the Baptist and asks him, "Who are you?" Behind that fake question was their real question, "Are you the Messiah?"

John is astute enough to know that and he tells them, "No, I'm not the Messiah, but he's coming. It's not me, but he's close by. I'm not worthy to tie his sandals, and he's right around here. He must increase and I must decrease, and he's coming soon, so get ready."

It's really easy to imagine John. Fiery-eyed, a camel hair shirt with a belt around it (in the heat of a desert summer even!), long unkempt hair and beard, a diet of locusts and wild honey. We would look at him today as a nutcase, but he was clearly excited about his faith. He's a great example to us about how we are supposed to be excited about our faith.

What happens when we go to Mass? We hear the Word of God and Jesus shows up in a big way in the Eucharist. But what do we do? We sit there with blank looks on our faces as if we were constipated, looking at our watches saying, "God, it's been forty minutes already." That's why John is a good example for us. He got excited, even in the womb!

The next day, after John has said he's not the Messiah, he sees Jesus walking towards him. In the last chapter I mentioned how John was pointing out Jesus to everyone else. Well, how do you think John was doing it? I don't think it was in a ho-hum kind of voice like, "Ah, behold the Lamb of God (yawn!). Yeah, that's the guy I told you about, the one who takes away the sins of the world. Good to see ya."

I think it was more like, "Look, look, look! *There* is the Lamb of God who takes away the sins of the world! That's the guy I told you about! Look at him!"

With all this excitement, what do John's disciples do? Nothing, absolutely nothing. It's not until the next day when John says it again that they do anything.

Here's a question for you, why, when John is going bananas trying to point out the Lamb of God who takes away the sins of the world, do his followers not do anything? Maybe it's because Jesus wasn't what they expected. Sometimes he isn't what we expect.

I think his disciples said, "Excuse me? That's the Messiah? But, John, he looks just like us. Look, he's wearing the same kind of clothes we're wearing, the same rough hands, the same kind of sandals. He looks just like us. Where's the sword? Where's the white charger? Where's the helmet? Where's the armor? He's going to lead us out of Roman domination? He's going to be our savior?" I think they were looking at him saying, "That can't possibly be the one we've been waiting for, the anointed one of God."

So when Jesus shows up again on the third day, I think John really goes berserk. I think he's jumping up and down saying, "There he is again! I can't believe he's back! Look, there is the Lamb of God!" And no one is doing anything. I think he gets frustrated and says, "I'm supposed to be the voice crying in the wilderness and you're just sitting there! Do something! You're embarrassing me."

John and Andrew are sitting in the crowd talking between themselves something like this:

"If he keeps this up, John's going to have a coronary."

"Yeah, he's just going nuts."

"Alright, let's get up and do something.

"OK, let's follow this guy."

They get up and start to follow Jesus just like I do – not too closely. I used to say, "Oh, I want to follow Jesus. I want to be just like those apostles. I want to be in his inner circle. But I don't want to get too close to him because if I get too close to him, he is going to do something and change my life. I don't want him to change my life. I like my life. I like my mess. Don't make waves."

When I read the Scriptures, I always like to put myself in the position of one of the characters. So what would I be like if I were John or Andrew while they were following Jesus? This is the way I imagine it. (By the way, this is no great theological reflection, only my imagination at work):

"Yea, there he is. I think he's taking a left, John. You go over by the tree. I'll meet you over there."

And they run over to the tree. "O.K., Andrew. He's taking a right by that boulder."

So they're following him, just keeping him in sight, like the Abbott and Costello of Scripture.

"He's going around that curve up there."

"Let's get behind that bush."

Jesus knows this is going on and I think he stops and thinks, "I'm just going to wait here for them in the middle of the road." And they come running around the bend in the road – and there he is, two feet in front of them. Oops.

"Hey! How ya doin' Jesus? Good to see ya."

And Jesus says to them: "What are you looking for?"

And then they ask this funny question: "Where do you dwell?"

What they mean is: "What are you about? Who *are* you?"

And Jesus, being the most loving, kind, intelligent man of all, gives them this answer: "Come and see."

Here is Jesus, fully man, but also fully God, the one who made everything that is, the Savior and Redeemer of the world, and he wants to be our friend. That's what he means by "come and see." "Come and find out. Come and spend time with me. I live in my Father's kingdom. Do you want to come and find out about that? Do you want to come and be my friend? Then come and see." That is what he was saying to them.

So John and Andrew stay with him for the day and they get to know him a little bit. If we want to be Jesus' disciples, we need to do the same thing – spend time with him. And we do that by praying in front of the Blessed Sacrament, taking time for prayer at home, reading the Scriptures and the teachings of the Church.

But above all, when we read his words and hear his voice, we have to do them. Jesus says, "Why do you call me 'Lord, Lord' and not do what I say?" If we don't do what he commands, then we've missed the point about being a follower of Jesus.

It's like the New Jersey farmer who gets visited by a Texas farmer, where everything is always bigger and better. And the Texan says, "Tell me about your farm."

Now, the New Jersey farmer is pretty proud of his farm. "Well, it's small, about 120 acres, 40 of that is pasture. I've got about 50 Holsteins that I milk, another 20 that are calving. The barn's pretty new, only about five years old, and it's got a milking parlor. I'm growing beans, oats, corn and alfalfa."

And the Texan's just looking at him as though he was the most pitiful creature on earth.

"Let me tell you about my place in Texas," he says. "When I get up in the morning and it's just starting to get light, I get in my truck and I start driving. Let me tell you something – I drive all day long. All day long I drive, until the sun is starting to set. And you know what? I'm *still* not to the end of my property. What do you think of that?"

And the guy from New Jersey, brightens up, looks the Texan right in the eye and says, "You know what? I know what you mean. I used to have a truck like that."

Well, sometimes it's not so bad to miss the point. But we can't miss this point: God loves us and he has given us the best he has – his Son, Jesus Christ, who took on our flesh, carried our weaknesses and sorrows, suffered, was crucified, died and rose from the dead and has given us the Holy Spirit for our salvation.

In following his commands and doing what he tells us to do, we get to know more about Jesus, we get to walk on a different street and not fall down holes, and that street will lead us to the ultimate point of life – being with God forever.

Chapter 13
Good News International

Around the time God started to ask me to come to work for him, I learned about these lay-run workshops on evangelization being held in Florida in the mid-90s. There were laypeople who were coming from all over the country to participate – lawyers, brokers, real estate experts, property managers.

These were exciting workshops. I was enthralled because I was hearing the Gospel being preached by laity for the first time. I came home and made Cheryl go and she took a group of people from the parish to one. Then I dragged my pastor, Father Brendan Williams, down there, too. He got excited about it and when he got back, the two of us went to visit our bishop. At that time, the Bishop of Trenton was Bishop John Reiss. He gave us his permission and blessing to do something along the same lines.

I was still in business and spending my own money promoting these workshops on evangelization. I would fly the people up from Florida to New Jersey to come give the seminars. They were a week long, lasting from Saturday to Thursday and people would come from all over the country. We would feed and house them and they would have access to all this wonderful teaching.

We wouldn't charge anything for this and people would give donations at the end of the week.

This went on for 3 1/2 years, and after a while, people would come up to the teachers and ask, "Would you come and do a mission for my parish?" But the teachers' response was, "Well, we're booked." Then they would turn to me and say, "Well, Bill. Why don't you think about doing it?"

After a while, I started to think that perhaps God was calling me to do this. Over the next few years, I started to do it part-time and go wherever I was invited.

At this time, I was really involved in my community. I had four businesses – a real estate company, a travel agency, an insurance agency and a building and development company. I was also the president of the board of education for my town and had my own cable television show. But I finally decided that God wanted me to work in the ministry full-time, so I got rid of my businesses, either selling them or giving them away, and I dropped the show.

Of course, along with everything else that comes with ministering full time, comes the consideration of money. We needed money for an office, personnel, travel and all that kind of stuff. But I had no idea where it was going to come from.

In the meantime, I met a guy by the name of Peter Grandich. You might remember him as the "Wall Street whiz-kid." Peter was the one who predicted the financial market slump of the late 1980s. He had recently become a Catholic and joined my parish. He became interested in the ministry and said that he would help us. How that help came about was something I could never have predicted.

Peter offers a newsletter about his services for his clients. Now this is a pretty pricey newsletter and it goes to a rather exclusive clientele. Part of the service includes an 800-number clients can call. They punch in a special code and get Peter's tip of the day on stocks – what to buy and what to sell.

One day, Peter called me to his office and said, "Listen to this." He keyed in the 800-number and it played a regular message to his investors regarding which stocks were hot and which were not. But at the end of the message, he said this, "Now I'm going to talk to you about something that has to do with God and religion. If you have a problem with that, hang up now." Of course, no one wanted to hang up.

"I have a friend," he told them, "who has given up his income and his businesses because he feels that he's been called by God to spread the Gospel. A lot of you have made a lot of money over the years listening to my tips. I've helped you, and I'm going to ask you to help me now. If you could, I would like you to send me a check to help out Bill Wegner."

I listened to that message and I thanked him and said, "Well, maybe we'll get some money of it."

A couple of weeks later, my phone rang at the ministry office. I picked it up and on the other end was someone who was obviously crying, and not just crying but sobbing. I couldn't tell who it was.

"What's the matter? Who is this?" I asked repeatedly.

Finally, this voice choked out, "This is Peter Grandich."

"Peter, what's the matter? Is everything OK?"

"Yes," he sobbed, "but I have all these checks for your ministry." He was completely blown away by the generosity of his clients.

But here's the kicker – most of the initial seed money for Good News International, a Roman Catholic lay evangelization ministry, came from Jewish investors from New York City.

About two years later, I had the unique opportunity to meet them. Peter had a seminar and he asked me to come. I told them all about the ministry and said to this mostly Jewish crowd, "Thank you for supplying the money to start our Catholic lay ministry." And they applauded and gave me a standing ovation.

That money helped us a lot to start preaching the Good News of Jesus Christ around the country and the world. Since 1994, we've done more than 300 retreats, parish missions and conferences in about 30 different states. Plus we've been to Central America, Ireland and Northern Ireland.

All of this is free of charge, and we live only on the donations of those who invite us to their parishes.

What has the impact been? Sometimes the results are hard to see, but sometimes they're not. Our missions are four-day events. It's easy to see the body language, particularly in the men, saying, "I don't want to be here" on Sunday night for the first talk. But by the fourth night, their hearts are softened and they're ready to receive the Word of God, Jesus Christ.

I've had people tell me they didn't want to come because, after all, "What can a layperson tell me?" But then within the next few days they come and tell us, "I haven't gone to Confession in 25 years," or "I talked to my sister for the first time in seven years," or "You gave me so much to think about," or "I never looked at Jesus this way," or " There's a guy at work who's a real pain in the neck to me. But you know what I did? I did something good for him and now he's like my new best friend."

These are what I call "mini-conversions." But there are some major conversions, as well. Here's what a young woman told me who stopped in by "chance" at a parish mission we were giving:

"Sunday night, I was on the way to kill myself. Actually, I stopped here just to say to goodbye to God.

But I came in and sat in the back that night. God used you to save my life. Thank you."

After another parish mission, an older couple came up to me. "We want you to know that your talk on forgiveness really touched our hearts," they said. "You see, three years ago, in front of her two teenagers, our daughter was murdered by the man she was dating. He's in prison now.

"Because of your talk, we are going to the prison next week to tell this man that we forgive him for killing our daughter."

The way these people responded, of course, has far more to do with the work of the Holy Spirit than it does with me or Good News International. But God chooses his instruments wisely knowing how to bring about his will. And for many people, that's a formerly wealthy real estate man from whom they hear practical ways to live the faith. Quite frankly, I think they can look at me and say, "Bill, if you can do it, I can do it."

Believe me, the only way I can do it is by God's work in my life. Without that, none of this would have been possible at all.

Postscript

"Be perfect, as your heavenly Father is perfect." Matt. 5:48

There was once a little monk renowned for his wisdom and holiness. He spent his days in prayer, writing and giving counsel to those who sought him out.

One day as he was writing in his cell, there was a commotion outside – raised voices, shouting, feet running, things clanging together. Suddenly, the door to his cell flew open and there was a knight standing before him. He had obviously just come from the battlefield and was covered with mud and blood, with holes in his chain mail and his armor all in disarray. Several monks were still trying to get him out, when the holy monk signaled to them to let the soldier be.

"Father," the knight said between his heavy breathing, "can you tell me what the difference is between heaven and hell?"

The little monk looked up at him and put down his quill. "Look at you," he said. "You've disturbed this whole monastery, this holy place. Who do you think you are to come charging in like that unannounced, tracking mud and dirt all over the place? Look at you. You look awful. You're disgusting. You smell. You're rude. Who do you think you are? Get out of my sight! I can't stand to even be near you."

Now the knight was completely taken aback by what the monk said. Here was a man who had a reputation for great holiness speaking to him in such a fashion. And he became so upset that he began to lose control of himself and, unsheathing his sword, raised it over his head and was about to strike the monk, when the monk said, "That, my son, is hell."

The soldier could not believe that this little guy was ready to give up his life to teach him a lesson. He slowly brought his sword down and put it back in its sheath. Realizing what he just learned, he began to smile, and the monk said, "And that, my son, is heaven."

How we respond to what happens in life is what makes a heaven or a hell out of it. Relying on God's grace to do as he commands us will bring us the happiness we so desperately need and want in our lives. Living without it and reacting, as the soldier did, out of our passions will bring us a living hell. It's up to us, then, to choose how we're going to live.

What I have tried to do in this book is to give you, the reader, some small idea of how you can become holy. Holiness is not something that is unattainable, out in the stars and only for a select few monks and nuns. In fact, one of the clearest concepts to come out of Vatican II was the universal call to holiness – every member of the

Church is called to be holy, whether we are married, single, religious, lay, diocesan priest, religious priest, deacon, nun, sister, monk or hermit. If you're Al, the high school custodian, you have the same vocation to holiness as does Mother Teresa, or the Holy Father or your Bishop.

That you have to become holy is not in question; Jesus even commands it. *How* you become holy is another issue.

If I were to ask 20 different people to define the word "holiness" I believe I would get 20 different definitions. From my experience of doing that, asking people what "holy" is, most of them would confuse the meaning of it with the word "pious." They seem to think that to be holy is to walk around with eyes cast downward and hands folded. The result of this misconception is that very few people admit to being holy. In fact, some folks vehemently deny being anywhere near holy. Teens are even worse. If you want to annoy a young person (and who wouldn't), say something like "I heard you're very holy." The response would be, "AAAAGH! NO! NOT ME!"

Well, I have news for you. You already are holy. You are holy by your Baptism; set apart for God and claimed for Jesus Christ! That holiness is affirmed and confirmed by our Confirmation through the power of the Holy Spirit working in our lives. Of course, we the Baptized and Confirmed have not yet reached the fullness of holiness. But at the very least we should know that we are on a journey…a journey to true and complete holiness

Here is how it works: Jesus is the complete package. No assembly is required and batteries are included. He calls us to holiness, models it for us, gives us all the graces and gifts we need to empower us (sacraments, Mass, adoration, prayer life,) and when we fall – and we will fall – Jesus picks us up, gives us more models to encourage us (the Blessed Mother, the saints, other people around us), loves us, forgives us, and sends us out again. That is what the Sacrament of Reconciliation is all about.

So, what is holiness? Holiness is truly **hearing** the Gospel, **grasping** it with our minds, **bringing** it into our hearts, and then **living** it out in our everyday lives. We are to be doers of the word not just hearers. "Be doers of the word and not hearers only, deluding yourselves. For if anyone is a hearer of the word and not a doer, he is like a man who looks at his own face in a mirror. He sees himself, then goes off and promptly forgets what he looked like. But the one who peers into the perfect law of freedom and perseveres, and is not a hearer who forgets but a doer who acts, such a one shall be blessed in what he does." (James 1:22)

There's an old proverb: "To hear is to forget. To see is to remember. To do is to understand." If we truly want to understand the Gospel of Jesus, we need to **DO** the Gospel.

Jesus mapped out our call, our vocation to holiness, when he sat down His disciples and gave them the Beatitudes: "Blessed are the poor in spirit, for theirs is the kingdom of heaven. Blessed are they who mourn, for they will be comforted. Blessed are the meek, for they will inherit the land. Blessed are they who hunger and thirst for righteousness, for they will be satisfied. Blessed are the merciful, for they will be shown mercy. Blessed are the clean of heart, for they will see God. Blessed are the peacemakers, for they will be called children of God. Blessed are they who are persecuted for the sake of righteousness, for theirs is the kingdom of heaven. Blessed are you when they insult you and persecute you and utter every kind of evil against you (falsely) because of me." (Matt 5:3-11)

This is Jesus' personality. He is poor in spirit, meek, hungry for righteousness, merciful, pure of heart, a peacemaker, and so on. This is Jesus. He calls us to be like him and then gives us His plan for our life: the Sermon on the Mount/Plain.

You see, the glory of God is not just found in a beautiful sunrise or sunset or in a miracle cure. The glory of God is also found in the everyday. We think a miracle is when we pray and God does what we ask. But another definition of miracle is when we pray and then we do what God asks.

The book you have just read is a frail attempt on my part to capture in the printed word what God has shown me about my call to be holy. I hope with all my heart that this book will encourage you in your vocation of holiness. But I also hope it will challenge you in your attempts to truly live a Christ-centered life. The old adage rings ever true, "indeed Jesus came to comfort the afflicted, but He also came to afflict the comfortable!"